THE SECOND MUST GO

A Manifesto for Revamping the Constitution of the United States of America

PIERGIORGIO L. E. USLENGHI

"A little rebellion now and then is a good thing"
Thomas Jefferson

authorHOUSE®

AuthorHouse™
1663 Liberty Drive
Bloomington, IN 47403
www.authorhouse.com
Phone: 1 (800) 839-8640

Published by AuthorHouse 11/10/2017

ISBN: 978-1-5246-9405-0 (sc)
ISBN: 978-1-5246-9404-3 (e)

Library of Congress Control Number: 2017908380

This booklet is dedicated

To my wife Shelly

To our children Amy, Silvia, Paolo and Raven

And to our grandchildren Spencer, Alistair,
Clayton, Clara, Julianna and Olivia

With the fervent hope that the
Amendments proposed herein

Be adopted during their lifetime

TABLE OF CONTENTS

INTRODUCTION

"The layman's constitutional view is that
what he likes is constitutional and that which
he doesn't like is unconstitutional"

Justice Hugo L. Black,
United States Supreme Court

As an immigrant who came to the United States from Italy in 1961, this country has offered me many opportunities – for work, for education, and for community life. It was a privilege to become a naturalized citizen in 1982. Most of my professional life has been devoted to teaching and scientific research in engineering, applied mathematics and physics – first at the Polytechnic of Turin in Italy, then at the University of Michigan in Ann Arbor, and for the past forty-seven years at the University of Illinois in Chicago, where I still work part-time after my retirement. So why would I want to write about revamping the Constitution of the United States?

During the fifty-six years that I have lived in the

States, I have observed the Civil Rights movement; the Cuban missile crisis; the assassinations of John and Robert Kennedy, Martin Luther King and Malcolm X; the war in Vietnam; the landing on the Moon; the opening to China; the impeachment of Richard Nixon; the hostage taking in Teheran; the reinstatement of the death penalty; the Soviet Union invasion of Afghanistan; the demise of the Soviet Union; the two Gulf wars; the disgracing of Bill Clinton; the HIV epidemic; the computer and communications technological revolution; the cloning of living beings; the rise of Islamic terrorism; the war in Afghanistan; the disaster of the so-called Arab Spring; the rise of ISIS; the gassing of civilians in Syria; the Russian invasions of Crimea and Eastern Ukraine; the proliferation of drugs and of homicides by firearms in our country; the acrimonious debates and legal fights over abortion, immigration and same-sex marriage; the ongoing nuclear threat from North Korea; global warming; the erosion of the purchasing power and standard of living of the American middle class; the election of Donald Trump and the consequent welcoming of the alt-right movement into Washington's inner political circles. To quote an ancient Chinese curse: may you live in interesting times.

All through those fifty-six years and until quite recently, a beacon of guidance and reassurance in the midst of political turbulence at home and abroad has been the conviction that Americans would always find a way to reach a sensible compromise among different viewpoints and move our country forward in the spirit set forth by our Founding Fathers when they drafted our Constitution. Americans used to be able to distinguish between the right of free speech and adherence to the law, and to accept the consequences of civil disobedience if such course of action was dictated by their conscience. In the 1960s, I objected to the war in Vietnam and took part in the March on Washington to protest such folly, but I also registered for the military draft. The birth of my daughter (with a consequent re-classification from 1A to 3A) saved me from ending up in South-East Asia with a decent chance that my bones would now be fertilizing a rice paddy. I never considered deserting my military duty just because I disagreed with the policies set up in Washington. In the last few years, however, I perceive that the national climate has changed and personal and partisan interests are now trumping (no pun intended) what is good for the country as a whole.

The demise of the middle class and the ensuing feelings of frustration and inability to control one's future have been a fertile ground for such movements as the Tea Party and the various white supremacist and anti-immigration groups. Political divisiveness and orthodoxy have resulted in a paralyzed Congress, where very few Representatives and Senators from opposing political views seem willing to engage in a civilized and mutually respectful dialogue to compromise and pursue a course of action that is best for our country. These conditions threaten the survival of our democratic institutions.

While no simple recipe exists for solving the complex socio-economic problems facing our Nation, I believe that a few of those problems can be ameliorated by revamping our Constitution, thus defusing some contentious issues that have distracted us from focusing on other urgent matters. Some of the nine constitutional amendments that are proposed herein are straightforward, such as abolition of the death penalty. Those dealing with gun control and abortion are bound to be divisive, but in my opinion are nevertheless needed. Enacting amendments related to the Electoral College, the President and the Congress will require a good amount of selfless behavior by entrenched politicians.

Not listed here are one amendment still in limbo – the Equal Rights Amendment, and amendments addressing what I believe should be fundamental rights in addition to life, liberty and the pursuit of happiness: the rights to food, shelter, medical care, and education for all Americans of all ages. Maybe some future generations will enact those; one can always hope…

The contents of this booklet represent my personal views only, not those of the University of Illinois or any other organization. Also, I emphasize that to envision needed upgrading to our Constitution does not require a degree in jurisprudence, only a dose of common sense, as Thomas Payne would say.

THE ELECTORAL COLLEGE

Democracy: government by the people,
especially rule of the majority
(Merriam-Webster dictionary)

Proposed Amendment: *The Electoral College is abolished. The President of the United States is elected by direct popular vote. If no candidate receives at least half of the votes cast, a second election shall be held within thirty days between the two candidates who received the highest number of votes in the first election.*

In the presidential election of November 2016, Hillary Clinton received almost three million votes more than Donald Trump, yet she lost the election in the Electoral College. This is not the first time that a President was elected without a majority of the popular vote, but it is the first time that such an anti-democratic result occurred with such a huge margin.

The present system for electing the President of the United States is not a direct election by popular vote. It is a two-stage election, in which the voters choose their preferred candidate, but in reality they authorize a body of Electors who will vote for President at the second stage.

The Electoral College consists of 538 members, called Electors. Each State is allocated as many Electors as it has representation in Congress: its number of Representatives (435 in total for the Nation) plus two Senators (100 in total); additionally, there are three Electors for the District of Columbia. That makes a total of 538, a simple majority of which, that is, a minimum 270, is needed to win the presidential election. States use different mechanisms for selecting the Electors, but with the exception of Maine and Nebraska where a proportional allocation is in place, most States have a winner-take-all rule, meaning that the presidential candidate who receives the most votes in a State is allocated all the Electors from that State.

In order to understand how such a mechanism may lead to an undemocratic result, let us consider a hypothetical confederation of three States: State A has nine million votes cast and nine Electors; States B and C have five million votes cast each, and have five

Electors each; thus, there are nineteen million votes cast and nineteen Electors. There are two candidates, one belonging to the Blue party and one to the Red party. The Blue candidate receives eight million votes in State A and two million votes in each State B and C, for a total of twelve million votes. The Red candidate receives one million votes in State A and three million votes in each State B and C, for a total of seven million votes. However, under the winner-take-all rule, the Blue candidate has only the nine electoral votes from State A and loses the election to the Red candidate, who has the electoral votes from both States B and C: ten in total. The possible combinations leading to an undemocratic election result are too numerous to consider when fifty States and the District of Columbia are involved, but the gist of the exercise is clear: the winner-take-all formula for allocating Electors may lead, and has in fact led, to undemocratic election outcomes.

It may be argued that the solution to the problem just discussed is to require that all fifty States and the District of Columbia allocate Electors on a proportional basis. While that change would ameliorate (but not solve entirely) the problem when an election is between two presidential candidates only, it would not solve the problem if more than two candidates are in the running.

Consider the case of three presidential candidates, and suppose that the election result is as follows: the Blue party candidate receives 48 percent of the votes (and 258 Electors); the Red party candidate receives 45 percent of the votes (and 242 Electors); the candidate of the independent Yellow party receives seven percent of the votes (and 38 Electors). Since none of the three candidates has the required majority of 270 electoral votes, the Yellow party makes the following offer to the Red party: we want the presidency, but you may have all the cabinet appointments – if you do not accept our offer, we will vote for the Blue candidate. The Red party accepts, and the result is a President who was supported by only seven percent of the voters, and a Blue party completely shut out of the government, despite having received the largest number of votes.

The situation is complicated further by the fact that Electors are not legally bound to support the candidate to whom they are pledged, leaving the door open to all sorts of political pressures and backroom deals. If the Electoral College were to be unable to agree on a candidate, then the decision would be made in the House of Representatives, where there would be no guarantee that consideration be given to the plurality of votes cast in the election. A President who has been elected legally but does not enjoy the support of a majority of the voters has trouble establishing his/her legitimacy in the people's collective mind and may find it difficult to develop consensus on crucial issues facing the country.

In conclusion, the Electoral College is an anachronistic, fundamentally undemocratic and potentially dangerous institution. While it is true that the word "democracy" is nowhere to be found in the Constitution, it is also true that our Founding Fathers were not democratic in the sense of our understanding of that word today. For example, the reference to "all men being created equal" meant for the Founding Fathers not all men, but all white male landowners. Women, poor people, indentured servants, Blacks, Native Americans and other minorities had few rights and certainly not the right to vote when the Constitution was written. Times have changed dramatically in more than two centuries since then, and citizens now demand that democracy and transparency be ingrained in our electoral process.

THE PRESIDENT: QUALIFICATIONS AND TERMS OF OFFICE

<u>Proposed Amendment</u>: *Any person who has been a citizen of the United States for at least forty years may be a candidate for President. Any President may serve only for one six-year term. Any person who has held the office of President, or acted as President, for more than three years of a term in which some other person was elected President, shall be considered as having completed a full term in office.*

The requirement that candidates to the office of President be persons born in the United States was inserted in the Constitution by the Founding Fathers in order to protect our country from infiltrators loyal to foreign governments. For example, the suspicion that someone born in the United Kingdom, if elected President, would bring the United States back under British control was a legitimate fear at the time our Constitution was written. However, such danger is now essentially nonexistent because of the checks and balances in our governmental structure.

On the other hand, the birth requirement has been used as a propaganda tool in the attempt to damage the candidacy of legitimate politicians. The so-called birthers movement tried to derail the candidacy of Barack Obama in 2008, by claiming that he was not born in the United States, despite a certified birth certificate from Hawaii. This false innuendo continued all through the eight years of Obama's presidency, and was used briefly by Hillary Clinton in her attempt to win the Democratic nomination in 2012. Donald Trump used it as a propaganda tool until recently, when he finally retracted the accusation. I suspect that many people joined the birthers propaganda because they could not stomach the fact that a Black person had been elected President – a sad commentary on racism in our country.

During the electoral campaign of 2016, questions were raised about the qualifications of Senator Ted Cruz for the presidency because he was born in Canada, albeit the son of American citizens. The issue was dropped only when it became clear that Cruz would not win the Republican party nomination.

The time has come to judge the qualifications of a citizen to become President on the basis of character, ideological program, experience and past performance, rather than on where that person was born.

The Constitution set thirty-five as the minimum age to qualify for the Presidency, at a time when life expectancy was much shorter and the machinery of government much simpler than at present.

For a person to possess the maturity, judgment and experience required of one of the most demanding jobs on earth, it would seem prudent to expect a President to be at least forty years old (John Kennedy and Barack Obama were in their forties when elected). Under the proposed amendment, anyone born in the United States would qualify for the Presidency at the age of forty, whereas a naturalized citizen would qualify after having been a citizen for forty years.

When Franklin D. Roosevelt died during an unprecedented fourth term as President, the country realized that limits needed to be imposed on the length of service of any person as President. The 22nd amendment, ratified in 1951, set the limit to two four-year terms. After that amendment, during the sixty-four years from 1952 to 2016, we have had eleven Presidents with an average term in office of 5.8 years.

In one of his first pronouncements after winning the Presidency, Donald Trump stated that he was looking forward to doing great things over the next eight years. While I do not recollect his exact words, the "eight years" mention struck a chord: here was a person who had just been elected and was already thinking about his reelection four years down the road. The need to act so as to maximize his chances for reelection was obviously of paramount concern to him. This is a problem with all politicians who are allowed to run for consecutive terms of office, but is particularly vexing for a President, who might have to make a hard choice between what is good for the country and what is good for his reelection. The only sensible solution seems to be to limit each presidency to a single six-year term, which is very close to the 5.8 average length of presidential service during the past 64 years, and which gives ample time to a President to enact his/her agenda without having it clouded by reelection concerns.

THE U.S. CONGRESS: ELECTION AND TERMS OF OFFICE

<u>Proposed Amendment:</u> **Section 1.** *A Senator from each State is elected every six years at the time of each presidential election. A second Senator from each State is elected every six years at the time of the midterm election, which occurs three years after each presidential election. Senators may serve for any number of six-year terms, but for no more than two consecutive terms. Any Senator who has filled a vacant seat for more than three years shall be considered as having completed a full term in office.*

Section 2. *All Representatives are elected for three-year*

terms, the elections being concurrent with the presidential and midterm elections. Representatives may serve for any number of three-year terms, but for no more than four consecutive terms. Any Representative who has filled a vacant seat for more than eighteen months shall be considered as having completed a full term in office.

In the early years of our Republic, public service was often an unpaid civic duty. Nowadays, Senators and Representatives receive a generous salary, a pension, medical care, and other significant benefits inherent to a powerful legislative position. Thus, service in Congress has become a well-remunerated, highly desirable career, whose members defend with ferocity their chance to serve. Some legislators put their own reelection interests ahead of the good of the country in their work, to the point that it has become difficult to defeat a sitting Congressman in an open election. Congress has become a sort of aristocracy, where elected people cling to their position for very long times and seldom relinquish it voluntarily. Unpaid service in Congress would be undemocratic, because only wealthy persons could afford to serve, and in any case it would not solve the problem of a lack of rotation in elected positions. Nevertheless, some revision to the present state of affairs needs to be made.

The amendment proposed herein would limit the continuous length of service in Congress to twelve years for both Senators and Representatives, while allowing them to reenter Congress after a one-term hiatus (six years for Senators, three years for Representatives) in order to loosen the stranglehold that many of them have on their elective position and to allow other citizens to serve. The present term of two years for Representatives is too short, and does not allow a newcomer the time to implement a legislative agenda before having to focus on the next election.

This amendment is interwoven with the proposed presidential amendment. The proposed election of half the Senate every three years would put all fifty States on an equal footing.

DEATH PENALTY

"Thou shalt not kill"
(Exodus 20:13)

Proposed Amendment: *The death penalty may be imposed only for national security during a declared war or a declared natural catastrophe.*

In the Spring of 2015, while in Riyadh, Saudi Arabia to recruit graduate students for the University of Illinois at Chicago, I found a public beheading announced in the local paper. The execution, which of course I refused to attend, took place in a downtown public square. The object of this barbaric event was an Indonesian woman who had been hired by a local wealthy family as a servant. After a prolonged period of mistreatments by the lady of the house where she worked, she had apparently become mentally ill and, in a moment of rage, had killed the young son of her mistress. In Saudi Arabia, a person guilty of murder can escape execution if pardoned by the family of the victim, but the pardon usually follows only after a sizable financial compensation has been received by the victim's family. In conclusion, rich offenders may escape capital punishment, but poor offenders are doomed.

Before feeling smug and more civilized than the Arabs, let us look at some recent executions in the United States. The current way to kill condemned people is by lethal injection. However, various States have encountered difficulties in securing the drugs needed for killing people in cold blood, and have had to resort to alternative drugs, often with tragic results. As an example, the drug Midazolam is responsible for at least four cruel executions; in 2014, two executions in Arizona and Ohio resulted in prolonged agony for the prisoners, who were gasping for breath; Clayton Lockett died after his execution was botched and stopped in Oklahoma; in December 2016, Ronald Smith in Alabama heaved and gasped for almost fifteen minutes before dying. Only a sadist would deny that such executions constitute a cruel and unusual punishment.

The United States is the only Western country in which the death penalty is still applied. The death penalty is admissible in thirty-one of the fifty States, by lethal injection. In some States and under certain conditions, the person on death row may select a different manner of execution: electrocution in Alabama, Arkansas,

Florida, Kentucky, South Carolina, Tennessee and Virginia; gas inhalation in Arizona and California; hanging in Washington; firing squad in Utah. Details may be found in "Capital Punishment in the United States" and references therein, in Wikipedia.

Much has been written both pro and con about the death penalty. Advocates for the death penalty claim that it deters crime - if that were the case, the United States would not be the country with one of the highest rates of murders in the Western world. As stated in the *Chicago Sun Times* on April 27, 2017, "eighty-eight percent of American criminologists surveyed by researchers at the University of Colorado say the penalty is not a deterrent, while chiefs of police polled by R. T. Strategies, a public affairs group, said the death penalty was the least effective way to prevent violent crime".

In addition to its being a cruel and unusual punishment (which I believe to be the case, notwithstanding inaction on this matter by the Supreme Court), there are at least four other good reasons for abolishing the death penalty:

- The abolition would bring the United States back into the cradle of the civilized world. In the period from 2007 to 2012, only four countries carried out more executions than the United States:
  China, Iran, Saudi Arabia, and Iraq.

- The possibility of executing an innocent person would be eliminated. A few years ago, when it was discovered that Texas had condemned an innocent man to death, the prosecutor who was responsible for putting him on trial allegedly boasted that it takes a good prosecutor to convict a guilty person, but a great prosecutor to convict an innocent one!

- Accused people who cannot afford powerful and expensive defense lawyers often are represented inadequately by public defenders, resulting in rates of conviction and death sentences much higher than the average. For more than two centuries, poverty, prejudice and racial hatred have conspired to inflict capital punishment on minorities at a much higher rate than on the white majority, for the same crimes.

- The years (sometime decades) of appeals between the imposition of the death sentence and the execution cost the State millions of dollars. It would be cheaper to incarcerate the convicted person for life.

Those who still favor the death penalty need to be reminded that justice is not synonymous with revenge. To paraphrase the Mahatma Gandhi, "an eye for an eye will leave the whole world blind".

It must be recognized that there may be times in the life of a nation when extreme danger to that nation's survival during war justifies the imposition of the death penalty. That exception is provided for in the proposed amendment.

There may also occur a natural disaster of such magnitude as to induce Congress to impose martial law across all or part of the country. Such might be the case if a large meteorite were to hit the Earth, or if the Yellowstone volcanic caldera should explode.

GUN CONTROL

<u>*Proposed Amendment*</u>: *The second article of amendment to the Constitution of the United States is repealed. The United States Congress shall regulate the licensing and use of arms.*

I recently spearheaded a petition drive to put the wording of this proposed amendment as an advisory, non-binding referendum on the ballot in the Township of Oak Park, Illinois, where I reside. The drive was successful and the referendum was approved by slightly more than 64 percent of the 28,306 township voters who cast ballots in the November 2016 general election. My hope is that this successful referendum will become a harbinger of similar and much larger efforts to curtail the availability of guns at the national level.

The second amendment was consigned to benign neglect until a few decades ago. At that time, it was largely understood as an endorsement of the National Guard, but then some conservatives championed by Antonin Scalia and funded by the gun manufacturers began a campaign to allow individuals to have all the arms they wanted. So now people can have semi-automatic weapons with a large magazine capacity and rapid firing (also called assault weapons), whose only purpose is indiscriminate maiming and killing. These are weapons that belong only in the army, not even in the police force, let alone in the hands of civilians. Yet Congress refused to renew the ban on such weapons after the Sandy Hook massacre despite strong public support for such measure, because our Congressmen and Senators hid behind the Second Amendment for fear of retribution from gun manufacturers and NRA lobbyists at election time.

In Texas, students are now allowed to carry loaded pistols to class, despite the strong objections raised by local police forces. For what purpose will they use the guns? Kill the instructor if they do not like the grade they received? Also in Texas, visitors can open-carry guns in mental hospitals. In other places people can carry loaded guns to church - what is the purpose? To kill the pastor if they do not like the homily? In many inner cities, children are afraid to walk to school for fear of being shot. In 2016 the city of Chicago witnessed 762 homicides by firearms and almost 5,000 injuries, many of them serious. In a speech to the International Association of the Chiefs of Police on October 27, 2015, President Obama pleaded for tighter gun controls and stated: "Just to give you a sense of perspective, since 9/11, fewer than one hundred Americans have been murdered by terrorists on American soil – 400,000 have been killed by gun violence. That's like losing the entire population of Cleveland or Minneapolis over the past fourteen years". More American civilians have died by gunfire in the past decade than all the Americans who were killed in combat in the Second World War (*The New Yorker*, June 27, 2016). About 30,000 Americans now die by gunfire every year, roughly the same number who die in transportation accidents.

The murder rate in the U.S. is about five times higher than in other civilized nations, and that is partly due to the free availability of guns in this country. Sadly, many deaths by guns occur because of family quarrels, accidents or suicides, not in attempts to defend life or property. Guns have become a drug in our country, and some people have become hooked on it.

By contrast, after a massacre in 1996, Australia enacted a National Firearms Agreement that severely restricts the availability of guns (it requires a "genuine good reason" for holding a firearm license), resulting in a drastic drop of homicides and suicides. From 1979 to 1996, Australia had 13 mass shootings involving five or more victims; from 1997 to 2016, it has had none (*Journal of the American Medical Association*, June 22, 2016).

The NRA and similar organizations defend the free availability of firearms on several grounds. The statement that armed people will protect themselves from tyranny made sense two hundred years ago, but is a romantic nonsense in the 21st century. A "well regulated militia" was effective until the beginning of the Civil War, when regiments were formed in various States and sent to Washington to serve in the Union army, but was already obsolete at the end of that war, when formidable federal Army and Navy had come into existence. The militia mentioned in the Second Amendment was formalized as the National Guard in the early 1900s.

The belief that an armed mob could protect us from tyranny is naïve at best – such a mob would be more likely to install a tyrannical government than to protect us from one. The best protection from tyranny is a large, prosperous and well-educated middle class.

The statement that criminals will always find guns and therefore a law-abiding citizen should have free access to firearms for personal defense is also naive. How can someone carrying a weapon, either openly or concealed, protect himself or anyone from a drive-by shooting or from a massacre such as the ones in a Colorado theatre and an Orlando nightclub? Keep in mind the fact that many homicides by firearms occur during family disputes, and that many suicides (often not reported in the press) could be avoided if firearms were stringently regulated.

The statement that gangs in the inner metropolitan areas are responsible for most homicides glosses over the fact that many young people in our inner cities grow up with inadequate guidance, possibly in a single-parent home, are uneducated or poorly educated, are exposed to drugs, and have no job prospects – these are serious and complex societal ills that cannot be cured by simplistic solutions like arming everyone and sending more people to jail. Youth gangs, by one name or another, have existed since the beginnings of mankind; when I was growing up in Italy, fights between youth groups ended in bloody noses and bruised egos, but no one was killed because guns were not available.

In conclusion, none of the arguments put forward by the gun manufacturers and their mouthpieces like the NRA stand up to logical scrutiny. The Second Amendment could be left as is, an obsolete and historical piece of legislation, if Congress had the courage to protect the welfare of the people, to wit:

- Forbid the sale of assault weapons to civilians.
- Forbid the sale of guns at gun fairs.
- Forbid the possession of guns by mentally impaired persons.
- Require proper training as a condition for gun ownership.

- Require that gun owners carry insurance (as is done for vehicle owners).
- Create a national gun registry.
- Regulate the transfer of gun ownership.
- Allow local government units to regulate strictly the practices of carrying guns, openly or concealed, including a total ban on such carries. The last bullet point can be buttressed by an additional justification. I believe that the Supreme Court ruled in the past that if any regulation, no matter how well intended, results in discrimination, such regulation is unconstitutional. Since gun carrying has resulted in a much higher rate of homicides among minorities in many areas of our inner cities than in the average population, it should be illegal in those areas.

Since the gun manufacturers and the NRA have resisted even the most logical and sensible regulations on firearms, and since Congress has been unwilling to act, the only solution is to abolish the Second Amendment while mandating Congress to act. THE SECOND MUST GO!

The right to bear arms can exist, and does exist, in any society, but with stringent limits that vary from generation to generation depending on the needs of the time. For example, no sane person would consider allowing individuals to possess nuclear, biological or chemical weapons. Congress should be responsible for defining those needs as they change with time. The right to bear arms is not a fundamental and absolute right on a par with the rights enshrined in the Declaration of Independence: life, liberty and the pursuit of happiness.

ABORTION

Proposed Amendment: *The right to abortion shall not be infringed upon during the first five months of pregnancy. Thereafter, abortion is permitted only if the health of the mother is imperiled or the fetus is deformed.*

The word abortion does not appear in the Constitution (and does not appear in the Bible either). Thus, in the last half century the judicial system has had to issue rulings based on a sometimes nebulous interpretation of the balance between the right of a woman to control her body and the protection that should be extended to an unborn child, trying to divine what the Founding Fathers might have meant on a subject that they did not even consider. Inevitably, judges ended up by ruling on the basis of their own personal convictions, often a blend between their concept of individual liberty and their religious belief. Even though, starting from the decision on Roe vs. Wade and until now, the Supreme Court has been consistent in its support of a woman's right over her body, the issue has divided our Nation like no other in recent times. One of the most important and most frequently asked questions of any nominee to a position on the Supreme Court is what his/her position is on abortion.

One extreme position on the issue is the tenet that even frozen sperm and unfertilized eggs are human life and should not be destroyed. One is reminded that in the Middle Ages, sometimes people caught masturbating were burned at the stake by the Catholic Church. Most pro-lifers hold to the more moderate position that a fertilized human egg is life and therefore should not be destroyed.

At the opposite extreme are the pro-choicers, who claim that a woman has the right to terminate a pregnancy until the very last moment before the child is born. This may result in crushing the skull of a perfectly healthy and fully developed infant who could survive on its own without medical assistance if separated from the mother – a practice that most people would classify as murder.

Thus, the fundamental question is at which point in gestation is an unborn human to be considered an individual person, separate from the mother and entitled to constitutional protection.

There obviously is no agreement on this issue, and any proposed solution is going to leave a segment of the population dissatisfied. It seems to me that a reasonable compromise is to consider the fetus as a separate human being at the time when it is able to survive without medical assistance if separated from the mother. Most doctors will agree that such is usually the case during the sixth month of pregnancy, hence the language in the proposed amendment.

FEDERAL LAW AND RELIGIOUS BELIEF

<u>*Proposed Amendment*</u>: *In the event of conflict between federal law and religious belief, federal law prevails.*

Since the early days of humankind, people have attempted to understand our universe in logical terms by inventing some transcendental structure that could explain such phenomena as creation, life, and good and evil. Such theoretical structures are useful in mitigating anxieties relating to our inevitable death by instilling the hope of eternity of the soul, or resurrection of the body, or reincarnation, and so on. Thus, religions were born, and they were often used by governments to control the masses, at times leading to theocracies with tyrannical consequences. The Inquisitors of the Catholic Church in the Middle Ages, and the present Ayatollahs of Iran and Kings of Saudi Arabia come to mind.

In order to treat all citizens equally, irrespective of their religious belief or lack thereof, it is wise to separate the affairs of state from religious affiliation.

Our Founding Fathers established a clear separation between Church and State, and some degree of separation between the religious and the secular worlds has since been implemented in all truly democratic forms of government.

Freedom of religion is guaranteed by the First Amendment. When the Bill of Rights was ratified in 1791, the prevalent religions were the various branches of Christianity, from Roman Catholicism to Protestant sects, and Judaism. Now we have not only the Manitou of the Native Americans, but Buddhism, Confucianism, Shintoism, the various divinities of the peoples from India, Allah of Islam, the Mormon faith, Scientology, Animism, etc. Anyone who is sufficiently narcissistic and possesses a gift of gab can invent a new cult that, if followed by a number of people for a sufficiently long time, gains the respected label of religion. All those transcendental mythologies are protected by the First Amendment. It follows that anyone may demur to abide by just about every law on the grounds that the law in question conflicts with a tenet of his/her religion. In recent times, we have heard of pharmacists who refused to dispense morning-after pills and of county clerks who refused to issue marriage licenses to same-sex couples, because of the respective religious imperatives the pharmacists and clerks held.

If a person were to enroll as a volunteer in the U.S. Army and then refuse to handle a weapon on religious grounds, that person would be discharged from the service. The situation would be different if there were a military draft and some recruits would raise conscientious objections.

If a pharmacist and a county clerk do not intend to fulfill the obligations of their freely chosen profession, they should choose a different career path and become instead a plumber, an electrician, an accountant, a teacher, or a florist. If they persevere in defying the law, they should be deprived of their licenses or removed from their official positions.

Religious belief has been used successfully not only by individuals to avoid legal obligations, but also by faith-based companies that have refused to support birth-control insurance for their employees.

The proposed amendment makes it very clear that people cannot freely select a profession and then abide only by the legal professional obligations that they like, choosing to hide behind some religious tenet. It will also protect the government from abuses by corporations that use religious freedom as an excuse to avoid paying medical insurance for their employees. Finally, it will screen the judicial branch of government, all the way to the Supreme Court, from the burden of frivolous litigation.

EDUCATION AND HEALTH

Proposed Amendment: *United States citizens and legal residents under the age of twenty-one years are entitled to free education and free medical care.*

The United States is one of the richest countries on the planet, and yet in 2016 one of every six American children went to bed hungry. The concentration of wealth in the hands of a small class of plutocrats, combined with the erosion of purchasing power by the middle class, will lead to the destruction of our democratic system of government unless remedial action is taken.

While there are neither sufficient resources nor political will to fix all societal problems at once, we should start somewhere. The most logical place is to concentrate on the welfare of the newer generations, because our children are the future of our country and of the world. We cannot let them die because of inadequate medical assistance, and we cannot condemn them to a substandard life by wilting their young brains through a lack of nutrition or education.

The cost of medical care is prohibitive for most individuals and families, unless they receive some employment or government assistance. To level the playing field, it is logical to provide free medical care to all citizens and legal residents of our country until they reach the age of twenty-one years.

Education, and particularly higher education in colleges and universities, has become so expensive as to be unaffordable by most middle-class persons. Families and individual students often have no choice but to borrow substantial amounts of money to finance education, resulting in debts that may take years, even decades, to repay. If free access to education were to be provided to all citizens and legal residents under the age of twenty-one years, young people would be able to graduate from high school and complete two years of college studies or trade schools without financial burdens. The long-range benefits to the country would be enormous. The cost of obtaining a bachelor's degree would be cut in half. The cost of getting an associate degree from a community college would be negligible – we would no longer have to import thousands of carpenters, plumbers, electricians, welders and health-care aids to fill the well-paying jobs that our country needs to fill. Equally important, we would nurture the expansion of an educated and financially stable middle class.

NATIONAL LANGUAGE

Proposed Amendment: *The federal language of the United States is American, a derivative of the English language. In addition to American, individual States may require the use of other languages in the conduct of state business.*

The Constitution contains no mention of an official, national language. Despite numerous attempts, Congress never approved an amendment declaring English as our national language.

As of now, twenty-seven States have passed official language laws. In 1923, Illinois declared that American, not English, was the official state language, but later reverted to English. The distinction between American and English is an important one, because the two languages that were originally identical have diverged over more than two hundred years, and are becoming more and more different with the passage of time.

Some organizations, such as the American Civil Liberties Union (ACLU), object to a national language on the ground that it denies equal protection under the law and therefore would be unconstitutional. I find it difficult to justify such an objection, because all U.S. born citizens are supposed to learn American in school, and all foreign-born persons should have at least a rudimentary knowledge of American as a condition to become naturalized citizens. The proposed amendment gives each State the opportunity to adopt other official languages in addition to American, in order to accommodate the needs of residents of that State.

The American language, and its parent English, are tremendous tools to foster democracy, because they address all persons in the same grammatical manner, independently of social status. When I was growing up in Italy, I had to address my teachers and all adults outside my family using the formal "lei" form, while they addressed me using the familiar "tu" form. I considered that a put-down. In the English-speaking world, one uses the "you" form to address all persons, from a child to a lowly laborer to the President of the United States. The use of a single grammatical form instills into the human brain the notion that all persons are created equal.

If the proposed amendment were to be adopted, I would envision Congress charging the Library of Congress with the official task of creating and periodically updating an official American Language dictionary.

CONCLUSION

After the inclusion in 1791of the ten amendments comprising the Bill of Rights, our Constitution has been amended only seventeen times in 225 years. The amendment process is a laborious one, and rightly so: one does not want to modify easily and without due deliberation what is arguably the most remarkable and enlightened legal document ever written. Most attempts to amend the Constitution have failed; for example, there have been some five hundred unsuccessful attempts to change the Electoral College, and recurring unsuccessful attempts to adopt a national language.

There are only two ways to change the Constitution. The first way is a Constitutional Convention which must be called by at least two-thirds of the States (presently, by at least thirty-four of the fifty States). This method has never been invoked and does not appear likely to be used in the near future because it would call into question the entire Constitution, with unpredictable consequences.

The second way to change the Constitution is to have an amendment approved by at least two-thirds of both chambers of Congress, and then by at least three-quarters of the States (presently, at least by thirty-eight States) within a reasonable period of time – usually seven years. This is presumably the route that should be followed in securing approval of the amendments proposed herein. It is not an easy way – no matter how reasonable and even necessary, since some of the amendments will run into entrenched powerful interests, or meet with indifference.

As an example of how much time it might take to have an amendment ratified, consider the Equal Rights Amendment (ERA). It was introduced in Congress in 1923, passed by Congress in 1972 and sent to the States for ratification. However, only 35 of the required 38 States had approved it by the deadline of 1982 set by Congress. In March 2017, thirty-five years after that deadline, Nevada ratified the amendment. There is still a chance that the ERA might be added to the Constitution if two more States ratify it, but only if Congress agrees to extend the deadline. The twenty-seventh amendment, on congressional salaries, was first proposed in 1789 but ratified only in 1992, two hundred and three years later!

The nine amendments proposed in this booklet may be divided into three groups of three amendments each. The first group addresses the need to restructure the election and terms of office for the President and the Members of Congress. I consider the proposed changes to be important for maintaining democracy in our country.

The second group – abolition of the death penalty and of the Second Amendment, and regulation of the right to abortion – speaks to the protection of human life and individual rights. Of the three amendments in that group, the repeal of the Second Amendment has the potential of saving tens of thousands of lives every year. Its implementation is of great urgency, hence the title of this booklet.

The third group is concerned with establishing the supremacy of the law over individual creeds and opinions, with protecting and nurturing our youth, and with further unifying the country under the umbrella of a federal language.

If adopted, these proposed nine amendments would make us a kinder, more progressive, more democratic and more cohesive nation.

ACKNOWLEDGMENTS

I am grateful to my wife Shelly and to our friend Domenica Moroney for suggesting improvements to the manuscript.

An indispensable source has been the booklet by Terry L. Jordan, *The U.S. Constitution and Fascinating Facts About It*, Oak Hill Publishing Co., Naperville, IL. The quotes by Thomas Jefferson and Hugo Black are taken from that booklet. I have also extensively consulted the book by Lee Goodman, *Too Many Rights and Too Many Guns*, Professional Education Resource Corp., Northbrook, IL, many newspapers and magazines, as well as *Wikipedia.*

Printed in the United States
By Bookmasters